Travel

AND Tourism

KAYE STEARMAN

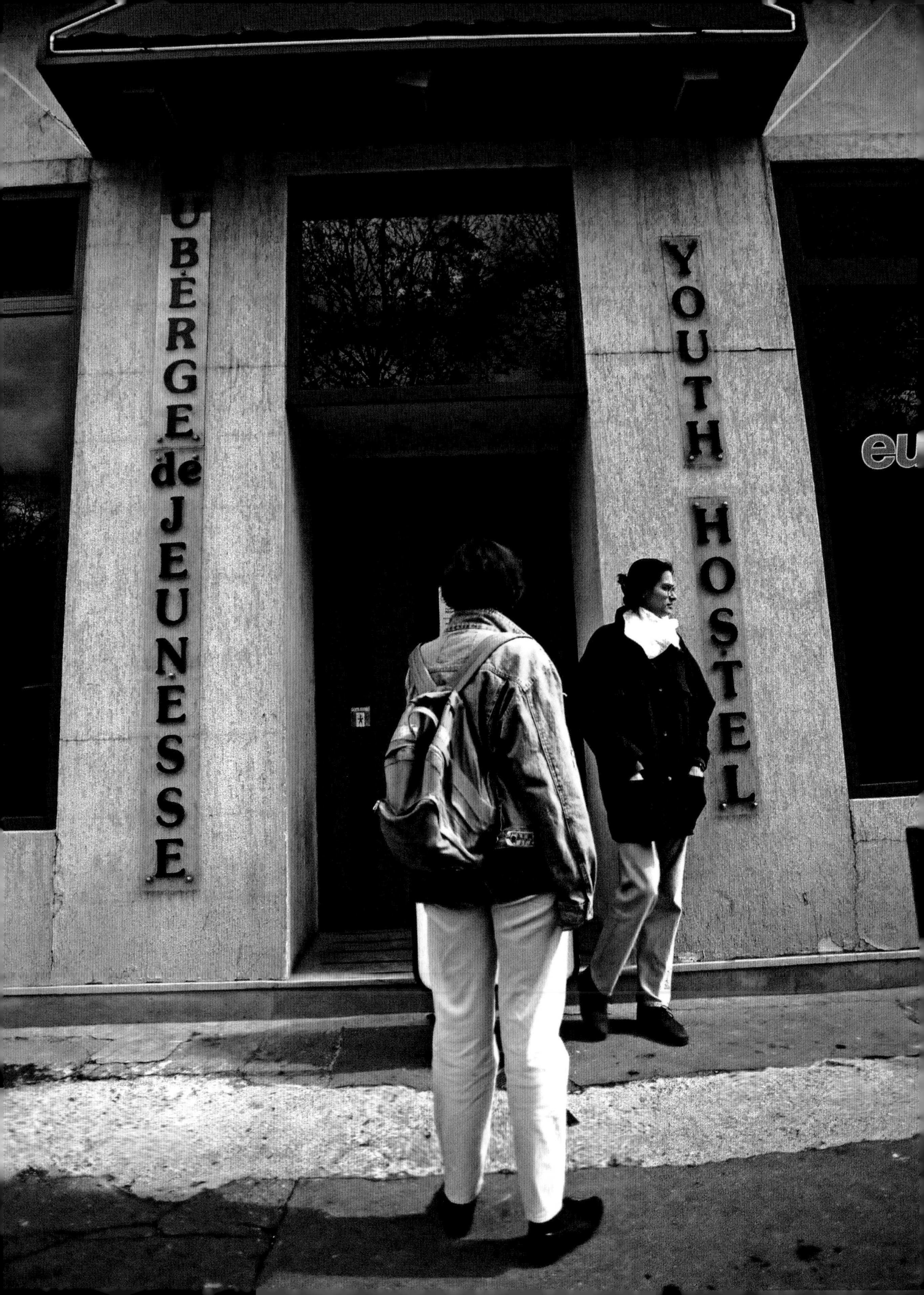
UBERGE de JEUNESSE
YOUTH HOSTEL

Contents

World on the Move

Today's tourism industry is much more than just travel. Tourism covers everything from older people on a day out to a family holiday at a beach resort, from a business executive on a overseas trip to a gap-year student on a long backpacking adventure.

TYPES OF TOURISM

The travel and tourism industry is generally divided into internal (or domestic) tourism and international tourism. Domestic tourism takes place within the same country and may be quite local. International tourism takes place in one or more countries.

Travel and tourism can be also be divided by sector. The largest sector, employing the most people, is personal tourism – people travelling for holidays and leisure. Business travel is a smaller sector but a higher value one. Business travellers tend to stay in more expensive hotels and spend more than tourists.

THE GROWTH OF TOURISM

Tourism has increased hugely over recent decades, aided by prosperity and the growth of road and air transport. The international tourist industry is one face of globalisation – the world coming together through faster communications and linked systems. People move more readily between countries for work and leisure; one of the key factors in international tourism is visiting family members abroad. Tourism is expected to grow still further in the coming years, although economic recession is likely to mean cutbacks in some areas.

Ready to see the world – a young woman traveller on a gap year prepares for the journey of a lifetime.

Despite its advantages, tourism can have a destructive impact. The more people travel by road and air, the more carbon emissions increase. If tourist numbers are high, they can bring about the pollution of natural beauty spots, the displacement of local people and an increase in the price of food and housing. In the worst cases, tourism provides income to undemocratic and corrupt governments who exploit and cheat their own people.

Tourism may bring benefits but it can also create pollution and waste. This beach strewn with rubbish is in the Dominican Republic, a popular tourist destination in the Caribbean.

CAREERS IN TOURISM

Because tourism is such a wide-ranging and ever-changing sector, you may not find it very easy to follow a defined career path. In general, large companies offer the greatest variety of jobs, travel and locations, and opportunities for advancement within the company. However, many people prefer working for a smaller company or running their own business, often in a specialist or 'niche' area.

For many tourism jobs the hours are long, pay is low and conditions are not always ideal. Jobs that involve extensive travel can be great for young, unattached people but not for those with family commitments. Nevertheless, the skills and experience gained prove to be extremely valuable to employers and can be transferred readily into other jobs.

FINDING A JOB IN THE TRAVEL AND TOURISM INDUSTRY

Many jobs are advertised online on travel industry and company websites. Look at the different jobs available and consider which best suit your skills. Consider taking a seasonal job first to give yourself a taste of the company and the industry.

Promoting Tourism

The tourist industry is big business. By spending money on food, accommodation, attractions and souvenirs, tourists support local businesses and jobs. Some businesses would not even exist without income from visitors. But tourism can thrive only if people know what an area has to offer.

GETTING THE MESSAGE ACROSS

It is not surprising that countries, regions, cities and towns make special efforts to attract tourists. Many have their own tourist organisation. Tourist information can often be found in kiosks in town centres and at airports and train and bus stations. Some of these outlets just provide information, such as leaflets and booklets, while others have staff who give advice, or book rooms or tours.

However, these are only a small part of the promotion effort. Tourism promotion involves training and supporting businesses and staff, preparing and checking information, and undertaking advertising and media work. In other words, it is almost an industry in itself.

TO WORK AS A PRESS OFFICER, YOU WILL NEED

●

communications skills, written and spoken

●

a keen eye for topics that are newsworthy

●

a qualification in, or experience of, journalism or public relations

FINDING A JOB – TOURISM PRESS OFFICER
For this job, you need to gain experience in similar roles in other areas and to take an interest in travel. It helps if you have done a bit of travelling yourself. On your curriculum vitae (CV) you should emphasise how the skills you have gained in previous work experience can transfer to travel and tourism.

This tourist office is located next to Reims Cathedral, one of France's great gothic buildings and a popular tourist attraction.

Part of the regular work of a press officer is phoning journalists and answering enquiries.

Janet – press officer

'I am a press officer for the city tourist authority. Our city is very scenic and has some beautiful and historic buildings so we are already well known. But we can't be complacent. Tourism is a very competitive industry and people will only come here if we can offer them good value and high standards. Although we have many tourists, they tend to come for only one or two days. We would like them to stay longer.

'As a press officer, I promote tourism through the media. I issue press releases and answer enquiries from journalists. I keep in touch with journalists to tell them of new developments, for example, a forthcoming exhibition or a new tourist attraction, and encourage them to feature our city in their publications. Sometimes we arrange tours for journalists or photographers.

'Last year we had a film crew shooting scenes in the city. I know that we will benefit from the extra publicity. I hope that when moviegoers see what a great place this is, more of them will want to visit.'

INFORMATION PROVIDERS AND WEBSITES

The internet enables people to search and book travel online, putting together their own travel and holiday packages. But websites also offer a valuable service by providing information for travellers, especially those seeking something unusual or different.

SEEKING INFORMATION

Perhaps tourists have an interest or hobby they want to pursue. They may be wary about food or hygiene at their holiday destination, or they may have special travel requirements. Today there are websites dealing with all aspects of travel, set up by tourism authorities, travel agents and enthusiasts. Many of these websites are interactive, enabling travellers to give their views on everything from the standard of hotel rooms and transport and prices to the friendliness of the local people. Tourists can draw on their own experiences and add comments to the websites, but much of the information is supplied by information officers.

HANDY HINT
If you are interested in becoming an information officer, think about how you can improve your research skills – through reading, using the internet and talking to people. Work experience with a voluntary organisation or charity may lead to a regular job.

MAIN TASKS – INFORMATION OFFICER

●

providing information by telephone, email and post

●

selling and sending out publications

●

updating website and information guides

●

giving quotations and making hotel bookings

●

dealing with membership enquiries and subscriptions

●

attending meetings and trade exhibitions

Electronic communication is a vital part of today's travel industry, especially for people with disabilities, who can browse information and opportunities from home or work.

Carrie-Ann – information officer

'Travel is one of my favourite things. I love the thrill of being somewhere new, full of people to meet. I enjoy the excitement of being in a strange place. But, as a wheelchair user, travel can be difficult.

'For most of my life I have travelled "mainstream" – booking hotels through a high-street travel agent, hobbling on to coaches, re-arranging furniture to accommodate my wheelchair. It wasn't until I started working for Tourism for All that I realised travel could be made easier.

'As an information officer, my main job is to share my knowledge about all aspects of accessible tourism and travel in the UK and overseas, from hotels to sources of holiday funding.

'I don't only act as an information officer for wheelchair users; I also work with people with other disabilities and medical conditions. Disabled people often only need simple adjustments or a bit of extra help but they may struggle to get people to understand what an important difference these relatively small changes can make. People with more complex needs have even more difficulties. I want to live in a world where tourism is really open to everyone.'

TRAVEL AGENCIES

Travel agencies sell services to business travellers and tourists. In the twentieth century, most travel was arranged through travel agents. And, although today many people book their trips directly via the internet, travel agents still provide an important service.

THE GROWTH OF TOURISM

With the development of mass tourism from the 1950s onwards, the role of the travel agent came into its own. For the first time, most people took regular paid holidays and had the money to journey further away from home. Travel agents offered a wide range of holidays catering for different tastes, at prices ranging from cheap package trips to luxury vacations. They could develop holiday itineraries, book transportation, hotels and tours, order foreign currency and advise travellers on matters such as visas and medical requirements.

Travel agencies operate in similar ways in most of the world – this agency is in Germany.

TO WORK AS A TRAVEL AGENT, YOU WILL NEED

● *an interest in travel, people and places*

● *good listening and customer service skills*

● *good IT skills, including an understanding of specialist travel systems*

● *budgeting and financial knowledge*

Travel agencies are usually commercial organisations, often part of a large company or chain, but they are also independent businesses. Many have outlets in busy shopping areas. Customers can pop in, look through brochures and ask staff for advice. For many people this is still the best way to arrange a holiday. They like the personal contact and the opportunity to ask questions.

A good travel agent is interested in his or her customers and willing to spend time searching for the right choice for their needs. If things go wrong, the travel agent will need to deal with customer complaints or arrange a refund or compensation payment.

Young backpackers sit on the deck of a ferry travelling between the Greek islands. Some may be on package tours, while others have arranged their own travel.

THE INTERNET CHALLENGE

Today, although there are more travellers than ever before, there are fewer shop-front travel agencies. This is because the internet now provides the means for people to plan and book their travel online. Many travellers feel this gives them more control of the whole process. As a result, a lot of traditional travel agents have closed, while others operate online or as telephone services.

Will travel agents disappear altogether? Probably not, because many people will still seek personal service and expert advice from an agent. The internet will create many new jobs in the travel industry, especially those involving the building of websites, search engines and other IT-related developments.

WHERE WILL I BE?
With several years' experience of working in this field, you could be managing a team of travel advisers, setting up your own travel agency or using your travel industry skills in another customer service sector.

Working for a Large Company

**There are many types of companies involved in tourism.
Most are small specialist operators. However, the industry
is dominated by a few large companies, each with their own
transport, hotels and tour operations.**

CATERING FOR DIFFERENT MARKETS

The wide range of travel brochures and holiday websites on
offer suggests that there are many different companies, each
with its own name, logo and 'brand'. But many of these are part
of just one company or group of companies. By trading under
different names they can aim at different sections of the market,
such as family holidays, holidays for young single people or for
older people.

Some large companies have their own chain of travel agencies or
shop fronts, while others sell through independent agencies or
the internet. Some specialise in one area, such as long- or short-
haul flights, while others focus on package tourism.

*Large companies operate under
different names, each producing
their own range of brochures
aimed at specific markets.*

A large company offers a range of jobs. Here a tour manager on a cruise ship checks paperwork while the tourists under her charge take a sightseeing tour.

THE PROS AND CONS OF BIG BUSINESS

Large holiday companies employ thousands of people at all levels, from the booking office and the airport to the holiday destination. These are not just frontline jobs, dealing directly with customers; they also include support jobs, in administration, finance, IT and logistics, which underpin the company's many complex operations.

There are a lot of advantages to working in a large company. Such an organisation offers a wide range of jobs and opportunities for career advancement. It runs in-house training courses. Many large companies offer benefits such as insurance, health and pension schemes, and the opportunity to travel without charge or at a discount rate. Holiday reps and tour managers are provided with accommodation while they are away on work.

There are also disadvantages, however. Earnings may depend in part on commission, so the more holidays, flights or tours a staff member sells, the more he or she will earn. This suits some people, but not everyone enjoys the pressures of the commission system. Some people find working for a large company impersonal and unfulfilling.

Many jobs are seasonal, especially those of resort reps, and are likely to appeal to younger people looking for excitement and adventure rather than those wanting a regular career path. Hours can be very long and staff may have to work at unsocial times. However, despite the drawbacks, many people feel that the experience gained with a large company will support them in their future working life.

HANDY HINT
Refresh your CV to see what skills and experiences match the post you are applying for. Consider extra training or refresher courses to improve your skills. With a seasonal job, make sure you apply in good time – most companies recruit workers many months in advance.

Goa International is one of India's largest airports, serving hundreds of thousands of package holiday-makers from Western countries.

PACKAGE TOURISM

Package tourism is a particular type of holiday, consisting of transport and accommodation advertised and sold together by a company. Package tourism started in the 1950s, when charter flights began taking sun-starved tourists from northern Europe to the beach resorts of the Mediterranean.

HOLIDAYS MADE TO ORDER

The idea behind a package holiday is a simple one. The holidays are listed in a brochure (or today, on a website) with their dates, travel arrangements and prices. Prices vary according to the season, with the highest during the summer holidays.

Customers choose the package that best suits their needs: for example, facilities for children for a family holiday, sporting activities and a lively nightlife for young single people, and a quiet relaxed atmosphere for older groups.

WINTER SPORTS

Package holidays are not confined to beach resorts. Winter sports, especially skiing, make up an enormous seasonal industry at resorts in mountain areas. Many winter sports holidays are sold as packages, with the company organising travel, food and lodging, often in a chalet or guesthouse. There are a large number of jobs available, including chalet hosts, ski instructors, childcare assistants, drivers and resort managers.

Many employees are local people but others come from outside the area for the winter season. Chalet hosts are based in the chalet and look after between eight and 12 guests each, preparing breakfasts and evening meals, cleaning up, and dealing with any problems that arise.

The big attraction of the job for many chalet hosts is that most of their day is left free for skiing. Wages are not high but companies provide accommodation and food, and often include free ski lift passes, equipment hire and medical insurance.

TO WORK AS A CHALET HOST, YOU WILL NEED

●

good and varied cooking skills

●

an ability to deliver high-quality customer service

●

a mature and well-organised approach to your job

●

a hardworking temperament

●

a willingness to work long hours

Winter sports are a major industry in mountain resorts. These children are being taught by a ski instructor in a beginners course at a ski school in Austria.

IN THE RESORT

Holiday representatives (reps for short) based at the resort play a key role in package tourism, supporting and assisting holidaymakers with information and advice.

There are several types of rep, including customer-service reps (also known as family reps), club reps (for 18–30 year olds) and transfer reps (based at airports). There are also specialist roles, including children's rep (caring for children of between two and 12 years of age), overseas entertainers and resort manager who ensures the operation runs smoothly.

Working as a rep can be great fun but it is also hard work and takes the rep away from his or her home and family for months at a time. Many reps are young – the average age is 25 – and work only for a few seasons. Others continue for longer, perhaps moving into an administrative or managerial role in the resort or in the company's office.

Many holiday resorts, like this one in Menorca in Spain, lay on special entertainment events for children. Here a children's rep joins in the fun at a mini-disco.

TO WORK AS A HOLIDAY REP, YOU WILL NEED

●

appropriate qualifications – for example, a nursery nurse qualification to work as a children's rep

●

some work experience – customer service or sales is useful

●

a friendly and approachable manner

●

to be calm under pressure

●

number skills – you will be selling tours and dealing with currency

●

flexibility

●

a willingness to work long hours

A current passport, complete with necessary visas, is essential for most international travel. Immigration officials and check-in staff need to check passports, while hotel staff may also require passport details.

Tracey – holiday rep

'As a holiday rep, my work is organised around a weekly cycle, with the busiest period being "changeover day". Flights arrive and depart in the early morning. We take departing guests to the airport and direct the new arrivals to the coach. After a head count we set off to the resort, which is an hour away. On the trip in, I introduce myself to the guests.

'We drop guests off at their hotels. After the last drop-off, I get a few hours' sleep and a quick breakfast before heading to our base hotel for my first welcome meeting.

'I talk to the guests about the resort and the facilities and hand out information leaflets. I sell excursions and recommend cafés and restaurants. I deal with any complaints – these tend to be about unsuitable rooms or missing luggage. Then it's on to the next welcome meeting. It's a long day and we finish with a party for guests at a local bar. Luckily most days aren't quite so long.

'In the high season and school holidays I am responsible for between 70 and 90 guests, in low season there are far fewer. The main thing is to be available when needed. Some people need a lot of attention, while others I hardly see at all. I enjoy my job, despite the pressure!'

FLIGHT SPECIALISTS

Some large companies specialise in selling airfares, rather than package holidays. Many look like traditional travel agencies with shop fronts in big cities and with telephone booking services; others operate only though the internet.

LONG-HAUL FLIGHTS

Most of these companies sell long-haul flights, often to a particular area, such as Australia, Asia or Latin America. When it comes to buying expensive long-haul flight tickets, some tourists prefer to discuss their plans with a travel consultant and explain exactly what they are looking for regarding dates, routes, destinations and prices.

Some flight specialists buy up blocks of airline seats and sell them at lower prices than other agencies. They may be the first to know of special offers or new routes. If price is not the main consideration, they can look for more convenient options, such as flights that leave or arrive during the daytime rather than at night, or journeys with interesting or unusual routes. Flight specialists often book hotels or create packages to suit individual travellers.

MAIN TASKS – TRAVEL CONSULTANT

●

communicating with customers face-to-face, via telephone and email

●

finding flights and accommodation to suit customer requirements

●

making reservations, ticketing, calculating and taking payments

●

keeping up to date with airline information, prices, taxes, etc.

●

advising customers on travel, visa and medical requirements

●

sorting out any problems that arise

Long-haul flights to tourist destinations are an important sector of the travel industry.

Good geographical knowledge is vital for staff working in the travel industry.

David – travel consultant

'I work at a large travel company with offices in Europe, Australia and North America. We specialise in long-haul flights, although we also sell short flights and weekend breaks. We open six days a week on a shift system starting at 8 a.m. and finishing at 7 p.m.

'My customers are a mixture of young backpackers who want cheaper flights and generally don't mind unsocial timings or long transit times, and older, more affluent people who are willing to pay more for convenience and will often book hotels and tours as well as flights.

'I deal both with walk-in customers and telephone customers – it can be quite difficult juggling the calls. You have to be a good listener and pay attention to detail. You need to check names, prices, special requirements, insurance, visas and health requirements. Often I reserve a flight, so a customer can come back to book later. Most people book by credit card – it gives them better protection if something goes wrong.

'You have to be a traveller to do this job well and all the consultants here have travelled on at least two continents. We enjoy using our own experience to help other travellers.'

Working for a Smaller Company

Although large companies cater for the majority of people, most travel operators are medium and small companies. They do well because they can offer specialist services aimed at particular groups, using expertise based on their own knowledge, contacts and experience.

SMALL COMPANIES

The simplest type of company is a business owned by just one person, providing a limited number of services. More common is a business partnership (two or more people who are joint owners) or a company with between three and ten members of staff. Employees often work on a part-time or seasonal basis, with the owners joining in carrying out the business.

Many businesses stay small either because their market is limited or simply because they prefer it that way. The owners may have started the business because they are interested in a particular country or area, interest or hobby. They know their customers well and can provide a friendly and personal service.

A small company can offer a range of activities, such as kayaking, in a quiet location far from the bustle of the crowded resorts.

MEDIUM-SIZED COMPANIES

Some businesses increase in size to meet growing demand. Most remain specialists but broaden their appeal by adding new services, activities, accommodation or tours, or extending into new areas or countries. For example, a company providing walking tours may start to offer tours in other areas or add other activities such as mountain-biking or kayaking. The operators may decide to offer a greater range of accommodation, for example luxury hotels or campsites.

As a company grows, it will need to employ more staff and find more finance, either in the form of loans or by bringing in extra business partners. Eventually the business may grow so large that the owners decide to sell it to a larger company.

GETTING WORK

Finding a job with a small company is not always easy. Some are family businesses and rarely employ extra staff. If they do, it may be by word of mouth or personal recommendation.

A medium-sized company, employing between ten and 50 people, will recruit in a more formal way, through press adverts, the internet or employment agencies, and will look for specific qualifications or experience. There is more opportunity for career advancement in a medium-sized company.

A camping or motorhome holiday offers a different sort of break. This campsite is in northern Italy.

TO WORK FOR A SMALL COMPANY, YOU WILL NEED

●

good communications skills

●

a flexible and adaptable personality

●

a thorough and precise approach to your work

●

a willingness to learn on the job

●

an interest in travel and the specialist area

23

REACHING OUT TO CUSTOMERS

To survive in the competitive tourism sector, specialist operators have to market their services to potential clients. Unlike large companies, they cannot afford big-budget television or poster advertising, and are more likely to use brochures and websites. However, often the most effective marketing is based on recommendations by satisfied customers.

MARKETING MATERIALS

Brochures are important marketing tools for most travel operators, large or small. A good brochure should attract potential customers with interesting text and illustrations while providing essential information, such as travel dates and prices. Putting together a good brochure takes painstaking research and attention to detail.

Today most travel operators have their own websites. Sometimes a website replaces the traditional travel brochure but often it is provided in addition to a brochure. Unlike brochures, websites are not limited by space or printing costs and can easily be updated. Many operators send regular email bulletins to customers who sign up on their websites.

MAIN TASKS – MARKETING OFFICER

●

developing a timetable and budget

●

agreeing design of brochure and other publicity materials

●

assembling and checking information

●

writing text and sourcing photos

●

editing text and making sure it relates to the photos

●

organising the printing and distribution of the brochure to customers

Travel brochures on display at a travel agency. The brochure is a vital marketing tool for small companies.

The growing numbers of older people with extra leisure time are an important market for the travel industry.

Kate – marketing officer

'I work for a business that arranges holidays for older people. My most important task is to write our annual holiday brochure. This is posted to thousands of regular customers and distributed to potential clients at meetings and exhibitions.

'The brochure must contain essential information about our holiday centres and their facilities, together with theme weeks and price lists. We want each brochure to look different from the last, refreshing the design and using new text and photos. We operate to a strict budget, so can't be too extravagant.

'This year I began by holding informal meetings with some regular customers to see what they liked and disliked about our previous brochures. They told us that they wanted more information about our facilities and clearer details on prices. They also said the photos were too gloomy! So I have used their feedback to make changes this year, including cheerful photos.

'Overall, everything went very smoothly. The worst part is checking that all the dates and prices are correct. The last days are frantic and I heave a sigh of relief when the brochure goes to the printers and then on to the customers.'

SPECIALIST OPERATORS

Look through the travel pages of a newspaper or on the internet and you will find advertisements for a huge variety of holidays. Specialist or hobby magazines will feature travel operators catering for your interest. There are holidays for noisy steam train enthusiasts and for silent birdwatchers, for energetic mountain bikers and for relaxed yoga practitioners. Maybe you want an eco-holiday on an organic farm or an escorted trek across a mountain range. What about a luxury escorted safari or perhaps you'd prefer a road trip with your own motor home? Whatever your preference, there will be a travel operator who can offer just what you want.

Mountain biking is a relatively new area of activity. Some specialist companies arrange food, accommodation and luggage transport for their guests.

FINDING A JOB – TOUR OPERATOR

Search through specialist websites and magazines and contact companies in areas where you have an interest. Build up relevant personal or work experience in travel, for example as a guide or tour manager.

WHERE WILL I BE?

In a small company there are opportunities to take the initiative and quickly add to your skills. You could soon become a team leader in the office or, if you are interested in the activities side of the operation, you could be a guide or expedition leader. Ultimately you could end up running your own business.

Accompanied by a local guide, a tourist enjoys meeting a llama at Lauca National Park, Chile.

Luca – travel operator and manager

'I am the director of Llama Travel, a company that specialises in guided holidays in Latin America. I founded the company seven years ago with a colleague. At first Llama Travel operated solely in Peru, a country I know well. As the company grew, we added new destinations in Ecuador, Chile and Argentina. Our aim is to offer good-value interesting holidays in a socially responsible way that benefits customers and local people.

'Today Llama Travel has around 2,000 customers a year, and employs nine staff in its London office. Staff responsibilities fall into three main areas – communicating with customers, usually by telephone or email, communicating with suppliers (airlines, hotels, etc.), and company administration, including finance or IT. While most staff focus on set tasks, it is important that they can do a variety of jobs.

'When recruiting staff, I look for experience of Latin America, together with the appropriate skills. Most of my staff are graduates. On a personal level, a staff member must be well organised, have good IT skills, be flexible and able to communicate with customers and suppliers. I encourage staff to contribute to the company by developing new destinations and services.

'My job is to oversee the business as a whole and ensure that it is financially stable and meeting our business objectives. It is much more than a nine-to-five job. I find it very satisfying to know that we have built a company based around my knowledge and love of Latin America.'

Getting There

People travel to their destinations in many different ways. Some use their own vehicles, especially for shorter distances or if they have a lot of luggage. But millions of travellers rely on mass transport, such as trains, buses, ferries, ships or planes.

TRAINS AND BUSES

Good transport facilities and services are vital to tourism. Not only do they transport millions of people to their destination, they are an industry in their own right and employ staff at all levels of the transport chain.

We all know of the frontline staff – from the ticket sellers and information staff at stations and booking offices, to the on-board staff such as drivers, guards, stewards and ticket inspectors, who operate our trains and buses. But behind these groups are the largely hidden backroom staff. It is they who inspect and maintain the vehicles, equipment and facilities and operate the complex systems that run and monitor the transport networks. Many of these jobs are highly technical and require specific qualifications and specialist training, through apprenticeships, or college or university courses.

A train is cleaned at the main station of Madrid, Spain's capital city.

Passengers expect good food and service when on a pleasure cruise. Here waiters remove used dishes as passengers relax on the sun deck while cruising on the River Danube in Europe.

TRAVELLING BY WATER

In some areas, for example, between Britain, Ireland and Europe, or between the Nordic and Baltic countries, ferries are an important means of transport. In general, these are fairly short trips, sometimes only a few hours. However, because ferries can carry hundreds of passengers they have many on-board services, including catering, retail and entertainment, all of which offer job opportunities.

Cruise ships provide a different type of service – a holiday afloat. A cruise may last from a few days to several months, but most cruises last two or three weeks. With ferries, the main aim is to get passengers to their destination quickly and in reasonable comfort; but with cruise ships the focus is on visiting scenic destinations, and providing entertainment and high levels of service. A large cruise ship may have hundreds of passengers and an equal number of crew and service personnel. However, many of these jobs are filled by professional cabin crew on long-term contracts and the opportunities for casual or seasonal work are limited.

FINDING A JOB – IN THE TRANSPORT INDUSTRY
Think about whether you are willing to work shift patterns or spend periods away from home. Research the different jobs available and the qualifications needed. Consider any apprenticeships and in-house training on offer.

AIR TRAVEL

Without air travel, the tourist industry would be very different. People would not be able to travel quickly and safely to holiday destinations far from their home. Thousands of tourist businesses – hotels and guest houses, cafés and restaurants, guide services and tour companies – would not exist.

CONTROVERSIAL ISSUES

Air travel is a controversial subject. Supporters say it is vital to the world economy, playing an important part in global business and tourism. Critics argue that planes are a major source of carbon emissions, which contribute to global warming. They also say that communities situated near airports suffer because of the noise and traffic pollution they produce.

What is not in dispute is that airlines and airports employ large numbers of people. For example, in 2008, London's Heathrow, the world's busiest international airport with 68 million passengers a year, employed 72,000 people. Around half these workers lived locally; others travelled in from further afield.

TO WORK AT AN AIRPORT, YOU WILL NEED

●

good team-working skills

●

a strong customer focus

●

an awareness of safety issues

●

a thorough and precise approach to your work

●

quick reactions, to cope with unexpected situations or emergencies

●

to pass a criminal records check (if working airside)

Los Angeles World Airport caters for both national and international flights and is one of the world's busiest transport hubs.

One of the greatest tests of an airport is its capacity to unload and transfer passenger luggage quickly and securely.

JOBS AT THE AIRPORT

Large airports offer a huge variety of jobs. These include management, information, IT, security and safety services, engineering, maintenance and transport crew (both landside and airside), and retail staff in the many shops and services. In addition, there are staff who work for individual airlines, or for independent companies that handle business for several airlines.

Some jobs, such as those of airline pilot and air traffic controller, are highly technical and require specific qualifications. Other jobs vital to airport operations include loading and handling baggage and freight, helping to move aircraft to the right place for refuelling, and assisting in airfield maintenance. Many of these roles require experience gained from apprenticeships and on-the-job training. Others are more customer focused, such as check-in staff or customer service agents.

Working at an airport does not suit everyone. Airports operate long hours – often around the clock – and many staff work on a shift pattern, perhaps starting in the early hours or ending late at night, or on different days each week. However, many employees maintain that shift work is convenient and suits their personal or family needs.

Journalists from home and abroad gather to examine the security procedures at Beijing's new international airport in the run-up to the 2008 Olympic Games.

LANDSIDE AND AIRSIDE

Airports are divided into 'landside' – the reception area open to everyone – and 'airside' – the area open only to passengers who have passed through security and passport controls. Some staff work only landside but many have to pass from one area to another every day.

Airports work to strict timetables and are very security conscious. Staff receive training in safety and undertake security drills. They are expected to be disciplined and alert at all times. Strict timing and good teamwork are important, as one delayed plane can cause problems at the airport for hours afterwards.

WHERE WILL I BE?
Experience as a member of an airport's check-in staff may lead to a position as a check-in supervisor, managing a team.

MAIN TASKS – AIRPORT CHECK-IN STAFF

●

checking passenger details and tickets

●

allocating seats

●

ensuring passengers know their boarding time and gate

●

implementing security procedures

●

ensuring help for disabled and other passengers needing special assistance

●

checking passenger details at the boarding gate

Anita – airport check-in worker

'I work at the check-in for a company that provides services for several foreign airlines. One day I may be dealing with business passengers bound for Asia and the next day with tourists headed for a beach resort.

'Many people think check-in is straightforward but our tasks can be complex. We need both IT and customer skills. Check-in counters open two or three hours before the flight is scheduled to depart and close 45 minutes before take-off. Sometimes queues build up, but we try to keep people calm and ensure the process moves along smoothly.

'We make sure the name on the passport matches that on the ticket and see that the passport and any visas are in order. We allocate seats and check that luggage conforms to size and weight restrictions. We ask passengers standard security questions, such as whether they have packed their luggage themselves and whether anyone has asked them to carry extra items. Then we fix tags to the luggage so that it can be routed through to the destination.

'Each day brings different problems. For example, one passenger's visa only became valid a day after her flight was scheduled to arrive, so I had to reschedule her connecting flight for the following day. Several passengers were delayed and were checked in at the last minute.

'After check-in closes, I go airside to the departure gate. We double-check passports and boarding passes. We oversee boarding, making sure that older and disabled people, and families with young children, board first. Our task is complete when all passengers have boarded and the flight is ready to depart.'

Check-in at the airport – friendly efficiency is key to a smooth service.

A Place to Stay

Business travellers and holidaymakers alike say that one of their top priorities is accommodation that meets their needs. Whether they seek a luxury hotel, a chain motel, a homely hostel or a beach hut, travellers expect their accommodation to be safe, clean, comfortable and convenient, and good value for money.

TYPES OF ACCOMMODATION

Large cities offer many types of accommodation. In smaller towns or in the countryside the choice is more limited, but prices are generally lower.

Chain hotels in large cities have the greatest numbers of rooms. These hotels are usually graded by the standard of facilities and services they offer – ranging from five-star luxury to the more basic two- or three-star establishments. Three- and four-star hotels are aimed at the business market, though many tourists stay in these too. 'Boutique' hotels are smaller luxury hotels with a more individual feel.

One- and two-star hotels tend to be smaller family-run hotels or bed and breakfasts (B & Bs), although these often have their own

A luxury hotel in Alexandria, Egypt, caters for business travellers and tourists.

TO WORK IN A HOTEL, YOU WILL NEED

●

to be good at customer relations

●

a calm, professional manner

●

a smart appearance, especially in front-of-house jobs

●

good IT skills – especially Windows, Excel, Fidelio (reservations systems)

●

financial and budgeting skills

●

good team-working skills

●

to be good at time-keeping

●

a willingness to work unsocial hours

A waiter knocks on a hotel room door as he delivers a room service meal order.

separate rating system. Motels are aimed at travellers who want a convenient stopping place at a modest price. Many motels are situated close to motorways or airports and some even have self-service check-in. Hostels are another budget alternative – they usually have some shared facilities, and are generally aimed at younger travellers.

WORKING IN A HOTEL

As with all large businesses, hotel chains offer many employment opportunities at different levels. For every staff member 'front of house' (directly dealing with guests) there are many more backroom jobs. Increasingly, jobs need specialist training and good IT skills; these qualities are especially useful for work dealing with reservations and payments. As with many other jobs in travel and tourism, hours can be long and sometimes unsocial.

Hotels chains usually offer in-house training and the opportunity to follow a career within the company. In a smaller hotel or hostel, work is likely to be less rigid and there is more opportunity to try out different roles. However, wages will probably be lower, jobs are more likely to be seasonal or part-time, and career opportunities are limited.

35

HOTEL CHAINS

Most hotel chains belong to large companies that own hotels in many countries. As with package tourism, one company may have several hotel chains, each with a different name and brand, and catering to different markets.

Hotel chains aim to offer the same standard of facilities and service at each hotel, wherever they are located. This means the guests should know exactly what to expect. Business travellers especially appreciate this environment as it offers no surprises and allows them to stay and work in a familiar atmosphere.

MAINTAINING STANDARDS

Staff working for a hotel chain are expected to maintain certain standards of appearance and behaviour and are given in-house training to ensure these are maintained. Staff members are issued with uniforms to reflect their jobs and name badges so they can be easily identified. In return, those who do well have the opportunity to learn different roles and be promoted within the company.

Hotel staff at a luxury hotel in Asia enjoy a moment of relaxation before guests arrive.

MAIN TASKS – FRONT-OF-HOUSE WORK

●

recording reservations and cancellations

●

checking in guests and allocating rooms

●

keeping tabs and drawing up bills

●

checking out guests and taking payments

●

dealing with sales and currency exchanges

●

dealing with requests, enquiries and complaints

Front-of-house staff provide a round-the-clock service to guests.

Jamal – assistant night manager

'I have worked for a leading hotel chain for five years. I started doing shift work as a student and got so interested in the hotel business that I decided that was where I wanted to work.

'For personal reasons, night work suits me. I worked for several years as a night auditor, managing the till and bill payments. The next step was as a reception shift leader, managing a small team. Last year I was promoted to assistant night manager.

'The night team takes over after the daytime management team leaves. We are there to keep all the services running smoothly. Some people think it must be easy work, but a lot can happen at night.

'Friday and Saturday nights are the busiest. Our banqueting rooms host parties and wedding receptions and guests often stay at the hotel, so people are going to and from the different areas most of the night. Generally it is just high spirits but sometimes things get rowdy – people may drink too much, or fights may break out, so we have to be ready to intervene.

'People also lose things – including their room keys – and some forget their room numbers. It's a matter of being tactful and diplomatic while keeping an eye out for any trouble that might develop. Safety and security have to be our number one priority.'

HOSTEL LIFE

Not everyone wants or needs to stay in hotels. Many budget travellers choose to stay in cheaper accommodation, such as hostels, bed and breakfasts (B & Bs) or in family homes, often called homestays.

YOUTH HOSTELS

The largest group of hostels, generally known as youth hostels, belongs to Hosteling International. Youth hostels started in Germany in 1909 to provide affordable accommodation for students on walking holidays. Today there are 90 youth hostel associations operating 4,500 hostels in 80 countries. Despite their name, most cater for people of all ages.

Youth hostels employ many young people on a seasonal basis and some employees go on to build careers in hostel management.

TO BE A GENERAL ASSISTANT IN A YOUTH HOSTEL, YOU WILL NEED

●

to be over 18 (most applicants are aged between 18 and 25)

●

common sense and an open cheerful personality

●

practical work experience, especially in housekeeping or catering

●

to attend youth-hostel-run open days for practical assessment tests

●

to pass police and other child safety checks

WHERE WILL I BE?

If you move up the career ladder in youth hostel work, you could rise to become a hostel warden. The experience gained from working in hostels will also qualify you for a hotel management post, or you could take the plunge and try running your own hotel or guesthouse.

Youth hostels like this one in Paris, France, provide budget accommodation for travellers and cater mainly for young backpackers.

Many youth hostels provide filling, nutritious meals for their guests and some also have self-catering facilities.

Chris – general assistant, youth hostel

'I am a general assistant at a youth hostel deep in the countryside. My day starts at 7 a.m. when we unlock the hostel and prepare breakfasts for guests. If we have a school party staying, it can be really noisy. We check-out departing guests and then spend the morning washing, cleaning and doing routine maintenance.

'The afternoon is usually free but I have to be back by 5 p.m. to re-open the hostel. I check-in new guests and allocate available rooms to them. The staff all pitch in preparing the evening meals – sometimes it's just for a few people, other times it's a full house. Once we have done the cleaning up, I often join the guests for a chat.

'The job has two main attractions for me. I love the countryside, especially as I am a keen birdwatcher. And I really enjoy meeting new people. Although we are a small hostel, we get visitors from all over the world. It really inspires me to travel myself.

'The downside is that the job is seasonal, normally eight or nine months a year, and the wages are not high. But accommodation and food are included and I can save quite a lot of my salary. It's great experience and a lot of trust is placed in you. As a general assistant you have to be very responsible and prepared to turn your hand to anything, but I don't mind – it makes life more challenging.'

Supporting Tourists

While some holidaymakers prefer to relax or party, others are keen to explore their new surroundings. While some are happy to use one of the wide range of guidebooks available, others prefer to rely on the expertise of a guide. There are many types of guides and their jobs are often seasonal. Tour managers tend to be employed to look after clients as part of their holiday package.

ENTERTAINING WORK

Tour guide jobs are available at theme parks, amusement parks, zoos and similar visitor attractions. Here the principal roles are service oriented, for example, helping customers, managing queues and entertaining children. Although these jobs can be quite low level, they provide experience and may lead to more permanent positions.

Eco-tourism is a growing sector of the tourist market. These tourists are looking for chimpanzees in the trees of Uganda's Kibale rainforest.

Some tours and cruises provide guides, generally called tour managers, as part of the holiday package. Other companies hire guides locally or recommend guides they know to be reliable. In many tourist destinations, guides offer their services directly to tourists, sometimes amid fierce competition for business.

A local tour guide with tourists in the French Quarter of the city of New Orleans, USA.

MAIN TASKS – TOUR GUIDE

●

assembling the group and assessing various people's needs

●

taking payments

●

leading the group and keeping good time

●

giving a lively commentary and answering questions

●

dealing tactfully but firmly with any difficulties

TOUR GUIDES

Tour guides are based locally and offer a variety of services. The simplest format is where a guide recites a standard commentary on a tour bus or boat. However, a good guide will provide a much more comprehensive service, tailoring each tour to the interests and capacities of his or her audience, answering questions and knowing what aspects appeal to different age groups and nationalities.

Walking tours, led by a specialist guide, are popular in many cities. These take place at fixed times and usually last between one and three hours, with between three and 15 people in each group. Walking tours tend to focus on a particular area, or specialist interest (for example, historic churches, literary life, industrial remains, or 'hidden history').

It is not easy to become an accredited guide in a major city such as London, Paris or New York. Guides need to be well educated and knowledgeable about a range of subjects, including history, art and architecture. Often they take extra qualifications and need certification from the local tourist authority. Guides have to be well spoken and articulate and able to deal with different groups of people with tact and humour.

Guides also need stamina to guide people in all weathers. Not surprisingly, most guides are older people who become guides after successful careers in education, archaeology or even show business.

A tour group treks on the Perito Moreno Glacier, Argentina, led by an expert tour guide.

MAKING A HOLIDAY MEMORABLE

A good guide does much more than simply show people the sights – he or she will make the tourist experience memorable. The visitor leaves feeling they have learned something new and interesting or seen familiar sights with new eyes.

TOUR MANAGERS

A tour manager is much more than just a guide. Tour managers (sometimes called couriers or escorts) are employed by the tour operator. In many ways, their role is similar to that of a holiday rep, except that they are not based in one resort and are constantly on call.

Tour managers travel and eat with their group and stay at the same hotels. The tour manager is in charge of the group's wellbeing throughout the holiday, ensuring that travel is safe, accommodation and food reach quality standards, and that customers receive what they pay for. The tour manager sorts out any problems that arise. If a guest falls ill or is injured, the tour manager makes sure the guest receives good medical attention, even if it means arranging for him or her to return home.

WHERE WILL I BE?

If the idea of becoming a tour guide appeals to you, it may well be that it suits your independent and free-wheeling temperament. You could continue your career as a freelance, choosing when to work, or you could end up running your own travel agency.

TO BE A TOUR MANAGER, YOU WILL NEED

●

extensive travel experience, including in difficult environments

●

a university degree in a related field (for example, geography or history)

●

a friendly and approachable personality

●

organisational, timekeeping and administrative skills

●

knowledge of, or fluency in, foreign languages

●

to be in good health, with lots of stamina

Anton – tour manager

'I have worked as an adventure tour manager for three years. At the moment I am based in Vietnam. I escort each group from the time they arrive to their departure two weeks later.

'Adventure travel is different from the usual escorted tour. Rather than just sightseeing, people sign up for an active holiday. So we go kayaking in Ha Long Bay, trekking in the Sapa Mountains, rafting on the Red River, and riding elephants through the jungle, all with local guides.

'After breakfast, I collect the group and we go by coach to our destination. I have briefed them the night before on what to expect and what to take – protective clothing, insect repellent and so on. After a morning hike past paddy fields and a visit to a local temple, we have lunch by the riverbank. Then we go by boat downstream to the village for our overnight stay. People have time to relax or explore before dinner and a display of local dancing.

'When I tell people about my job they think it must one long holiday – but being responsible for people's safety and welfare is no holiday, believe me! I also have to do a lot of paperwork, such as daily reports, accounts and incident sheets. Travellers pay good money for their tours so they want every day to be interesting and memorable.'

The experience of a lifetime – tourists take an elephant ride in Laos.

Further Information

BOOKS

Dale, Gillian **BTEC National Travel and Tourism: Books 1 and 2**, Heinemann, 2007

Espejo, Roman (ed.) **What Is the Impact of Tourism?**, Greenhaven Press, 2008

Evans, Sara **Real Life Guides: Travel and Tourism**, Trotman, 2008

Inskipp, Carol **Global Village: Travel and Tourism**, Evans Brothers, 2008

Kerr, Andrew et al. **BTEC National Travel and Tourism: Core and Specialist Units Books 1 and 2**, Longman, 2007

McAlpine, Margaret **So You Want to Work in Travel and Tourism?**, Wayland, 2008

Spilsbury, Louise **Ethical Debates: Tourism**, Wayland, 2009

Youell, Ray **Travel and Tourism For BTEC National Award, Certificate and Diploma, Books 1 and 2**, T and T Publishing, 2005

USEFUL ORGANISATIONS AND WEBSITES

www.bbc.co.uk/schools/studentlife/
The BBC Schools Student Life website. The careers and choices section contains summaries of different jobs, including qualifications and career prospects for some jobs in travel and tourism.

www.hihostels.com
Hosteling International: the site of Youth Hostel Associations worldwide.

www.hokey-cokey-jobs.co.uk/apply.php
A site giving details about jobs in YHA England and Wales.

www.syha.org.uk
The site for the Youth Hostel Association in Scotland.

www.tourismconcern.org.uk
Tourism Concern is a UK charity campaigning about the links between tourism, human rights, exploitation and pollution. Site contains resources for primary and secondary teachers.

www.tourismforall.org.uk
Tourism for All is a UK charity that aims to make tourism accessible, inclusive and welcoming to disabled people. Provides information and advice and a booking service.

www.wttc.org
The site of the World Travel & Tourism Council, a forum for chief executives of the world's hundred leading businesses in the travel and tourism industry. Very pro-business with statistics on tourism worldwide.

www.yha.org.uk
The site for the Youth Hostel Association in England and Wales.

Glossary

accessible when something is designed so that it can be used by disabled people, for example, ramps or wide doors for wheelchair users

apprenticeship a period of time, often several years, during which a person combines work with on-the-job and other training to qualify for a particular job (usually for younger people)

backroom jobs jobs that do not deal directly with the public

brand the 'identity' of a company – a brand includes things such as company name, logo and image

brochure a booklet with text and images outlining what a travel operator is offering its customers (for example, tours, hotels etc.)

carbon emissions carbon dioxide outputs caused by activities such as burning fossil fuels, deforestation and vehicle exhausts

chain a number of hotels and agencies with the same name and brand, owned by one company

commission payment made according to results, rather than as an agreed wage or salary

communications skills skills involving the ability to get your message across to others, usually through speaking or writing

compensation money paid to a customer or guests to make up for faulty goods or bad service

disability a physical handicap or learning difficulty which means a person may need some extra support to participate equally in society

eco-holiday a tourist venture that claims to aid the local environment or to have little or no adverse impact on the environment

exhibition a meeting where companies can exhibit their goods and services

freight goods carried by transport

frontline jobs jobs dealing directly with the public

front-of-house the first point of contact with the public, for example, the job of hotel receptionist

homestay staying as a paying guest in a family home

hostel a less expensive alternative to a hotel

insurance by taking out insurance, a person pays to protect against risk and receive compensation in case of injury or accident

itinerary a travel schedule

logistics developing, following and monitoring systems

logo an identifying symbol that is part of a company's brand

long-haul flights flights lasting five hours or more, often with one or more stopovers

marketing bringing a product or service to the public, for example through advertising or mailing a brochure

package holiday a holiday where the tour operator provides travel, transfers, accommodation and sometimes food as part of a travel package for a set price

partnership two or more people running a company

passport a document of nationality, usually needed for international travel

pension scheme an investment scheme where a company pays into an employee's retirement fund

police check an official check to see if a potential employee has a police record that might bar him or her from certain types of employment, for example work with children or vulnerable people

press release a short document issued by an company, usually to announce news or promote a new product or service

quality standards agreed standards of service and presentation, for example of rooms, facilities and food

refund a repayment to a customer who returns goods or cancels a service

representative/rep the representative of a travel operator or company whose main job is to look after a group of customers or guests

reservation an agreement to reserve a room or flight for a guest or customer

seasonal work work that is available only at certain times of year

short-haul flights flights lasting less than five hours

socially responsible tourism tourism based upon ethical principles; these might include a promise not to pollute or destroy the environment, or to support local employment

suppliers companies that supply goods or services, for example, hotels and airlines

visa a stamp or document in a passport that allows the passport holder to travel in a certain country

Index